Margaret Gee's
HEALTHY
ITALIAN
Cookbook

Margaret Gee's
HEALTHY
ITALIAN
Cookbook

TORTOISESHELL PRESS

First published in 1986 by
Tortoiseshell Press
Suite 221, Wingello House
1-12 Angel Place
Sydney NSW 2000. Australia.
Telephone (02) 221 1846

Design/Art by Ken Gilroy
Photography by Robbi Newman
Black and White Photography by Graham Monro,
Ross Honeysett and Marie Wielgosz
Typography by Begale Pty Ltd
Preparation of food for photography by
Margaret Gee and Elizabeth Brewer
Thanks also to the Italian Tourist Office and Alitalia

Dinnerware supplied by Royal Doulton,
Villa Italiana, Caposotto, The Waterford Shop,
Stanley Rogers & Son, R.P. Symons and Co.
Tiles supplied by Fred Pazotti
Posters by Polygram and Alitalia
Fruit and Vegetable Supplies by
George Zaide and Nick Khoury

Printed in Australia by Globe Press Pty. Ltd.

ISBN 0 947 063 01 3

Distribution by Gordon & Gotch (Australia)
Ltd. Melbourne, Sydney, Brisbane, Perth,
Adelaide, Launceston.

CONTENTS

Dedication

*T*his book is dedicated to my parents Kath
and Allan Gee, my brother Bruce, and my
twin sister Christine.

It is also in memory of Nathan Pritikin, and
for Mrs. Ilene Pritikin with gratitude.

"**P**RITIKIN STYLE ITALIAN FOOD – you must be joking." That was the response of a leading newspaperman when I announced my new cookbook idea. "You can't cook Italian food without olive oil, parmesan cheese, olives, eggs and cream," he bellowed.

"Can't," is a word that doesn't often turn up in my vocabulary. I have been cooking Pritikin style food for six years now, and my recipes embrace a wide variety of cuisines including Chinese, Italian, Japanese, Indian, Middle Eastern and others.

I have always believed it is more important not to compromise one's health than to worry about a miniscule compromise in taste. The essence of good cooking of any cuisine is to use fresh ingredients, fresh herbs whenever possible, and NOT to overcook the food.

This concept conforms well to the Pritikin principles, and is what European food is famous for. However, the Mediterranean countries like other Western nations have a high incidence of degenerative disease. Diets saturated in oil, fat, sugar and salt have prematurely claimed numerous lives and impaired many more.

Regardless of cuisine style, those culinary criminals – fat, oil, salt and sugar, – continue their relentless attack on innocent arteries.

With some simple modifications – Pritikin style – the same delectable taste sensations can be yours, without the harmful dietary effects.

Apart from extensive trips through Italy, I spent 11 years in Melbourne living close to the famous Lygon Street, Carlton. Lygon Street is Victoria's 'Little Italy'. This colourful street is alive with excellent trattorias, pizza and pasta speciality shops, and delicatessens.

It certainly was a great Italian culinary education to be in such close proximity to this 'delicious' part of the world.

Some years ago I travelled with my parents through Europe, and it was there that we all agreed Italian food was delectable and highly nutritious.

As you may be aware my father suffered three major heart attacks. His conversion to the low fat, low cholesterol Pritikin eating plan in 1980 saved his life.

Initially, like some others my father found the Pritikin style of food to be a little bland. However, once he realised that natural food cooked without oil, butter, salt or sugar CAN be exciting and tasty he has never looked back.

All the traditional famous Italian foods – pizza, pasta, polenta, vegetable, fish, chicken and meat dishes – even gelato CAN EASILY AND QUICKLY BE COOKED in the Pritikin style.

Italy is renowned for its comprehensive range of cheeses. Unfortunately, many of them contain too much fat and salt to be permitted on the Pritikin diet. But, the Italians do cook with ricotta or cottage cheese, so the low fat varieties can be used.

The recipes contained in this book are low in fat, cholesterol and protein, with no added salt, sugar or oil.

The recipes conform to the healthy eating principles outlined in the following bestselling books.

'The Pritikin Program for Diet and Exercise'
by Nathan Pritikin with Patrick M. McGrady.

'The Pritikin Promise – 28 Days to a Longer, Healthier Life'
by Nathan Pritikin.

'The Longevity Chinese Cookbook'
by Margaret Gee and Graeme Goldin

'The Health Revolution'
by Ross Horne.

'The Health Revolution Anti-Cancer, Anti-Heart Attack Cookbook'
by Ross Horne and Toni Bobbin.

I f one accepts the basic wisdom of the Pritikin principles of diet, and the number of protagonists grows daily (often without acknowledgement of their originator), then any information which helps adherence to that dietary idea is valuable.

A major requirement in all diets is the availability of hints to bridge the gap between conventional dietary habits and what is safe and worthwhile. It is here that Margaret Gee offers so much essential advice.

My present association with a major children's hospital has made me aware of two aspects of diet which may well be of even more importance ultimately than modifications of adult habits. Firstly, there can be no doubt that youthful diets lay the foundations of health or disease in maturity. Secondly, to design diets acceptable to children is a great challenge, in an age of fast and dangerous junk foods.

As in her Chinese cookbook, Margaret Gee has provided here a prodigious number of ways to adapt Italian recipes to safe states. Her industry is matched only by her skill and ingenuity. And all the while the information comes breezily, ever so clearly and attractively.

Margaret Gee is to be commended. I look forward to many more "international" contributions from her.

Professor John S. Wright
Associate Professor
Cardio-Thoracic Department
Prince of Wales Children's Hospital
Sydney. NSW. Australia.

IMPORTANT NOTE:

People who need to be on the Pritikin Regression diet should limit themselves to a maximum of 90 grams of animal protein per week; no more than three pieces of fruit per day, and completely eliminate dried fruit – as well as sticking to the limitations involved in the Pritikin Maintenance diet.

If you are on the Pritikin Maintenance diet eat only 84-112 grams of animal protein per day; a maximum of 680 grams per week.

I would like to take this opportunity to thank the hundreds of people who wrote to me complimenting me on the recipes contained in 'The Longevity Chinese Cookbook'. It was appreciated.

Sincere thanks are also due to the following people who provided me with so much valuable advice and support: Dr. Graeme Goldin, Morry Schwartz, Kevin Passmore, Celia Pollock, Barbara Goldin and Martin Dougherty.

Wishing you all good health and happiness – the two usually go together!

Buon Appetito

Margaret Gee

Margaret Gee

"WHAT CAN I EAT?"

The Pritikin eating plan recommends you use the following foods. The foods to avoid are also listed.

	RECOMMENDED	AVOID
ALCOHOL	Moderate use. Dry white wines are preferable	
BEAN CURD	Maximum amount allowed on Maintenance Diet 100 grams per day as a substitute for meat, chicken or fish.	
BUTTER	None	Margarine, all fatty dairy products.
CEREALS AND GRAINS	Wholegrain flours, breads, rice, spaghetti, other pastas	Any grain products containing added fat, oil, sugar, eggs, salt and non wholegrain products.
CHEESE	Small quantities of non fat ricotta cheeses	Full fat cheeses
EGGS	Egg whites only. Maximum 7 per week	Egg yolks, caviar
FATS/OILS	None	
FISH	Fresh fish, lobster, oysters, scallops or squid. Maximum amount allowed per day on the Pritikin Maintenance diet only 100 grams. This would exclude having any other animal protein during that day. On the Maintenance diet only, you can have 50 grams of prawns or crab per day, but NO OTHER animal protein during that day.	
FRUITS	Fresh only. Use only small quantities of dried fruits	Only use canned fruits if fresh not available. Buy those canned without added sugar. Don't eat fruit jams or jellies made with sugar or honey.

JUICES	Fresh fruit and vegetable juices	Processed canned or packaged. Fruit and vegetables are best eaten whole rather than juiced.
MEAT	Trim meat of all excess fat. Use only lean cuts. Regression diet: Eat only 90 grams per week Maintenance diet: Eat only 680 grams per week. (This allowance is for total animal protein – meat, chicken and fish consumed per week.)	Processed meats Salami, sausages Ham, bacon, offal, liver, kidneys, brains and other organ meats.
MILK	Skim milk only in small quantities Non fat yoghurt	Cream, whole fat milk, non dairy substitutes Commercial flavoured yoghurt.
NUTS	Chestnuts	All nuts *Small quantities of pine nuts are used in some of my recipes. People on the Pritikin Regression diet should avoid them.
POULTRY	Lean, skinned chicken or turkey	Duck, goose, pheasant
SALADS	Unlimited. Use only non oil, no added salt or sugar dressings	
SAUCES	Fresh only made without oil, butter, sugar, salt or monosodium glutamate	Commercial sauces with added oil, salt, sugar or monosodium glutamate
SEASONINGS	Use as per recipes	Monosodium glutamate, salt or sugar
SUGAR	None	Honey, molasses, glucose, sugar, syrup substitutes
TEA & COFFEE	Tea: Herbal teas are preferable Coffee: None	Decaffeinated coffee

COOKING UTENSILS

PRITIKIN recipes are easier to make if you use non stick cookware. Now that the health trend has accelerated non stick cooking equipment – fry-pans, saucepans, baking dishes – are widely available.

PASTA MACHINES – In my opinion the electric ones are over-rated and expensive. The same results can be obtained using a hand turned machine. Department stores and Italian shops stock these. Do not immerse in water. Before you rush out and buy one, decide if you are going to get your money's worth. If you're not, stick to buying the fresh or dried wholemeal pasta, which is relatively inexpensive.

LARGE COOKING POT – Required for cooking pasta, soups, steaming vegetables, braising meat, fish, chicken etc.

COLANDER – Necessary for straining pasta, vegetables etc.

GRATER – For nutmeg, low fat cheeses – 1% fat content only.

ELECTRIC BLENDER – Where would we be without them? If you don't have a blender a large mortar and pestle is useful.

BAKING DISHES – Useful for lasagne, cannelloni, and many other baked dishes.

SLOTTED SPOON – Ideal for removing gnocchi from the saucepan.

CHOPPING BOARD – A large sturdy board is excellent for efficient chopping of everything – vegetables, fresh herbs, meat, chicken, fish etc.

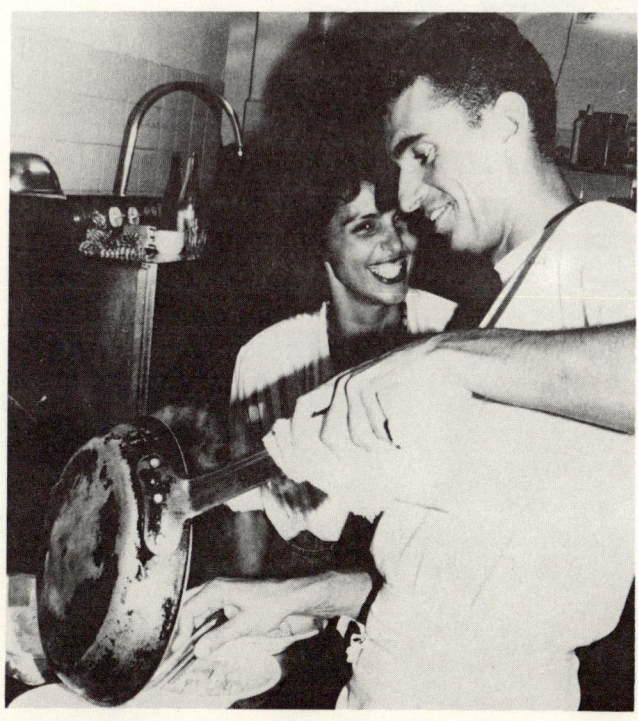

ITALIAN INGREDIENTS

F resh is best could well be the motto of any self respecting Italian kitchen. The emphasis on fresh vegetables, herbs, fruit, fish, chicken and meat can't be stressed too much.

Italian cooking like so many other cuisines varies from region to region, but there are some basic ingredients you might like to stock up on.

In general, the ingredients listed below will be available at your local super market, green grocer or Italian delicatessen.

BAY LEAVES: Bay leaves add a real Mediterranean flavour to soups, casseroles and other dishes. I often pop one into the water I am boiling for pasta. Remove before serving.

BEANS: Beans are frequently used in Italian dishes. They are essential for making hearty soups, and marvellous for main course vegetarian meals. The most popular varieties are borlotti – pink or red in colour; and cannellini beans which are white – similar to haricot beans. Tinned or dried can be used. Rinse tinned ones in cold water to remove excess salt, and drain. The dried beans require soaking overnight in cold water, or for two hours in hot water.

DRIED MUSHROOMS: These are popular for Italian sauces and soups. The flavour is quite strong, and you only need small quantities. They need to be soaked for 20 minutes in hot water before use. The best known variety is porcini, available at Italian delicatessens. If unavailable use fresh ordinary mushrooms.

FENNEL: This unusual vegetable has an aniseed flavour. It is delicious lightly steamed, baked or raw. Remove green tops and outer part of bulb first.

GARLIC: The mere mention of this word causes some people to recoil. To others – like me – its taste and fragrance is cherished. It is not used in ALL Italian dishes. If preferred it can be dispensed with altogether. There are many other delicious herbs which will give your Italian cuisine an authentic flavour. My advice is to use garlic according to the taste buds – especially yours – you are aiming to please.

HERBS

OREGANO, SAGE, THYME, MINT, MARJORAM: These herbs are used to flavour a variety of dishes. Try and obtain them fresh. If unavailable, the dried ones will have to do. They are easy to grow at home in small pots or in the garden.

NUTMEG: This spice is often used in dishes that contain spinach. If you want a really zesty nutmeg taste, buy whole nutmegs and grate it yourself.

PARSLEY: Italian parsley has flat leaves, but the curly variety is fine. Avoid using dried parsley.

PINE NUTS: These nuts are from pine cones. They are included in pesto – basil – sauce. Available in supermarkets, Italian shops, and health food stores. Use in small quantities.

PEPPER: If possible alway grind your own pepper as the flavour is greatly enhanced. I always think commercially ground pepper looks and tastes like house dust.

RADICCHIO: This crisp bitter sweet salad vegetable has dark red leaves. It is sometimes called red chicory.

RICOTTA: This soft, white, bland cheese is made from the whey not the curd of milk. It is a low fat, crumbly cheese used in many Italian dishes. It can also be eaten with fruit or salad.

Low fat cottage cheese can be used as a substitute. Ricotta does not keep for more than 2-3 days in the refrigerator. It is now sold fresh at many delicatessens.

SAFFRON: This is often used in rice dishes. Real saffron is expensive, and you need to soak the strands in a small amount of warm water first. When the water turns yellow, strain it, and add to your recipe.

TOMATOES: Try and use fresh ones. If you use tinned ones, rinse under cold water to remove excess salt.

TOMATO PASTE: Many tomato pastes are loaded with salt. Fortunately some unsweetened, salt free varieties are now available. Adjust quantity according to taste.

VINEGAR: Red or white wine vinegar is recommended. Malt vinegars are rarely used.

WINE: There are some superb Italian wines. Dry white wine, vermouth and small amounts of dry marsala can be used.

Selection of Italian Antipasto

Various Pasta Sauces –
Tomato, Mushroom & Ricotta,
Garlic & Parsley, Pesto (Basil)

Chicken Cacciatore and Herbed Croquettes

Above: Two of the smaller urns in GB Piranesi's 'Vasi' series of 1778, with a typically bold use of ox-skulls and gryphons, from Stephanie Hoppen. Opposite: Large urn by Piranesi, c1778; a three-dimensional etching which emphasizes the elaborate handles, from Lucy Campbell.

The Renaissance rediscovery of ancient monuments, and a new poetic attitude to the past, imbued antique vases with a special aura. Poliphilus's fantasy *The Hypnerotomachia* lovers wander in symbolic and broken vases, while in 1550, Enea Vico and publishing fine engravings bronze and marble vases their own in making Antiquities useful, an important source for print makers of the

ITALIAN REGIONAL COOKING STYLES

I talian food clearly expresses the colour, creativity and enthusiasm Italians are renowned for. Italian cuisine is as varied as the background, culture and geography of the nation.

But, whether you are after simple, rustic peasant food or sophisticated flavours Italy can please all palates.

It is one of my favourite countries. I adore good food, opera, music and art – and Italy is a treasure trove of all these pleasures.

As you will soon discover Italian food offers not only pasta and pizza, but much, much more. An Italian friend of mine once said: "Margaret, I don't eat to exist, I exist to eat."

Italian food is a delight to cook, serve, and eat – so what are we waiting for . . . ?

Minestrone Soup and Polenta

ANTIPASTO AND SOUPS

Antipasto refers to the appetisers Italians often serve before the main course. It can consist of a number of delicacies depending on what is seasonally available.

I recommend a combination of marinated vegetables or seafood, cannellini or borlotti beans, ricotta cheese, or even a slice of freshly baked wholemeal pizza. Thinly sliced roast beef or chicken can also be served.

Antipasto is often followed by either a light soup – brodo – or a heartier soup such as minestrone. If you serve a substantial antipasto, and minestrone with wholemeal bread it can be a satisfying meal.

The antipasto/soup combination also fits into the Pritikin idea of 'grazing' – eating several small meals each day rather than a 'hog heaven' indulgence three times a day.

TUSCAN TOMATOES
Pomidoro alla toscana

3 cups tiny ripe tomatoes
1 tablespoon fresh oregano finely chopped or
1 teaspoon dried oregano
1 tablespoon finely chopped fresh parsley
1 clove garlic finely chopped
2 tablespoons unsweetened orange juice
1 cup unsweetened orange juice
freshly ground black pepper to taste

Combine all ingredients and marinate in refrigerator
for 1 hour.

Serves 4-6

MUSHROOMS WITH GARLIC AND PARSLEY
Funghi all'aglio e prezzemolo

500 grams button mushrooms thinly sliced
3 cloves garlic finely chopped
1 purple onion finely chopped
½ cup red wine vinegar
½ cup fresh lemon juice
½ cup finely chopped fresh parsley

Marinate all ingredients for 1 hour and serve.

Serves 6-8

RENAISSANCE ROCKMELON
Meloncino Rinascimento

1 ripe rockmelon peeled and cut into small chunks
1 clove garlic finely chopped
1 bunch fresh basil finely chopped
1½ cups unsweetened orange juice

Marinate all ingredients in refrigerator for
1 hour and serve.

Serves 4-6

DELICIOUS ASPARAGUS
Asparagi deliziosi

1 bunch fresh asparagus. Trim off tough end pieces.

Dressing:

1 cup unsweetened orange juice
1 tablespoon fresh lemon juice
1 tablespoon red or white wine vinegar
1 tablespoon finely chopped fresh oregano or
1 teaspoon dried oregano
freshly ground black pepper to taste

How to cook asparagus is a contentious issue. Some people bring a large saucepan of water to the boil; tie string around the asparagus, and drop it into the boiling water for 15-20 minutes. I usually add a bay leaf to the boiling water and drop the asparagus in minus the string – for 10-12 minutes. Strain off water in a colander. While the asparagus is steaming it continues to cook. Allow to cool, and sprinkle with dressing just before serving.

Serves 4

CALABRIA CALAMARI
Calamari alla calabrese

500 grams calamari – washed and cleaned
½ cup fresh lemon juice
1 clove garlic finely chopped
2 tablespoons finely chopped fresh parsley
freshly ground black pepper to taste

Cut calamari into 1cm – ½ inch rings.
Bring a large saucepan of water to the boil.
Immerse calamari. Reduce heat and simmer for
10 minutes. Remove calamari from saucepan and allow
to cool. Combine with other ingredients and
marinate for 1 hour.

Serves 4-6

GARLIC/POTATO CRISPS
Patatine fritte all'aglio

4 large potatoes washed and peeled
4 cloves garlic finely chopped

With a potato peeler or sharp knife finely slice potatoes.
Slices should be almost transparent.
Place potato slices with garlic in water to cover. Put in
freezer for 5 minutes. Drain off water, and dry potato
slices with kitchen paper.
Preheat oven to 200°C-400°F. Put slices on rack
in baking dish and bake for 15 -20 minutes
until golden brown.

Serves 4

MINESTRONE SOUP
Minestrone

2 cloves garlic finely chopped
2 medium onions finely sliced
1 cup finely chopped celery
3 carrots finely sliced
2 zucchini finely chopped
3 fresh ripe tomatoes finely chopped
3 tablespoons tomato paste
4 cups defatted chicken, beef or vegetable stock
1 cup cooked brown rice
3 cups cooked dried beans – borlotti or cannellini
2 tablespoons finely chopped fresh oregano or
2 teaspoons dried oregano
freshly ground black pepper to taste

Place onion and garlic in large saucepan with 2 cups of
stock. Simmer covered for 5 minutes. Add all other
ingredients to saucepan except fresh herbs, rice and
pepper. Simmer covered for 30 minutes.
Puree half the soup in blender. Return blended soup to
saucepan. Add fresh herbs and pepper. Simmer for 5
minutes. Serve hot with wholemeal bread.

Serves 4-6

PAVAROTTI POTATO AND ONION SOUP
Minestra di Pavarotti, patate e cipolle

Unforgettable Pavarotti. I will always remember that
marvellous spectacular with Dame Joan Sutherland
and Pavarotti at the Opera House. This soup is good for
your vocal cords, and the rest of you!

5 medium onions finely sliced
8 medium potatoes peeled and roughly chopped
4 cups defatted chicken, beef or vegetable stock
1 cup skim milk
2 cloves garlic finely chopped
freshly ground black pepper to taste

Garnish: Finely chopped fresh parsley

Place onion and garlic in large saucepan with 2 cups of
stock. Simmer covered for 5 minutes. Add all remaining
ingredients and simmer for 30 minutes.
Puree in blender and serve.

Garnish with parsley

Serves 4-6

ZUCCHINI SOUP
Minestra di zucchini

750 grams zucchini roughly chopped
2 medium onions finely sliced
1 clove garlic finely chopped
3 medium potatoes peeled and diced
½ cup diced celery
3 cups defatted chicken, beef or vegetable stock
1 cup skim milk
1 tablespoon finely chopped fresh rosemary or
1 teaspoon dried rosemary
freshly ground black pepper to taste

Place onion and garlic in large saucepan with 2 cups
stock. Simmer covered for 5 minutes. Add all other
ingredients except rosemary and pepper. Simmer for
30 minutes. Puree half the soup in blender.
Return soup to saucepan. Add rosemary and pepper
and simmer for 5 minutes.

Serves 4-6

TOMATO AND BASIL SOUP
Minestra di pomodoro e basilico

4 cups defatted chicken, beef or vegetable stock
3 cloves garlic finely chopped
2 medium onions finely chopped
1 kg fresh ripe tomatoes roughly chopped
3 tablespoons tomato paste
1½ cups finely chopped fresh basil. Remove stalks
freshly ground black pepper to taste

Simmer onion and garlic in 2 cups of stock covered in
large saucepan for 5 minutes. Add all other ingredients
except basil. Simmer for 30 minutes. Puree half the
soup in blender. Return to saucepan. Add basil.
Simmer for 5 minutes and serve.

Serves 4-6

SPINACH SOUP
Minestra di spinaci

1 bunch fresh spinach. Remove stalks
2 cloves garlic chopped
1 medium onion finely sliced
3 cups defatted chicken, beef or vegetable stock
1½ cups skim milk
1 teaspoon freshly grated nutmeg
½ cup finely chopped fresh parsley
freshly ground black pepper to taste

Wash and finely chop spinach. Place garlic and onion
in large saucepan with 2 cups of stock. Simmer covered
for 5 minutes. Add all other ingredients except nutmeg
and pepper. Simmer for 20 minutes. Puree half the
soup in blender. Return blended soup to saucepan. Stir
in nutmeg and pepper. Simmer for 5 minutes and serve.

Serves 4

CAULIFLOWER AND RICE SOUP

Minestra di cavolfiore e riso

2 medium onions finely sliced
4 cups cauliflower flowerets
2 ripe medium tomatoes roughly chopped
5 cups defatted chicken, beef or vegetable stock
2 medium potatoes peeled and diced
1½ cups cooked brown rice
1 tablespoon finely chopped fresh parsley
1 tablespoon finely chopped fresh basil
freshly ground black pepper to taste

Combine all ingredients except basil, parsley and pepper. Place in large saucepan and simmer covered for 30 minutes. Puree half the soup in blender. Return to saucepan. Add basil, parsley and pepper. Simmer for 5 minutes and serve.

Serves 4-6

PASTA AND PIZZA

Pasta and Pizza are two of my favourite foods. They are ideal as a starter, main course or snack, and the range of toppings and sauces is extensive. Follow the instructions carefully, and you will be delighted at the tasty results.
A friend recently asked me how often I ate pasta.
I answered: "As often as possible!"

Spaghetti with Tuna & Celery Sauce

Assorted Pasta Shapes

PASTA

Whenever I think of pasta I think of Pavarotti – because he looks as if he eats a lot of it! Actually, pasta is NOT as fattening as you might think. What really stacks on the weight are the eggs, cream, butter, cheese, and oil which is usually used in such copious quantities.

The Pritikin diet is high in complex carbohydrates, and wholemeal pasta is an important item in the Pritikin eating plan.

In Italian shops, delicatessens, and restaurants wholemeal pasta is appearing more frequently – hooray!

When it comes to pasta you have a number of options: You can buy it freshly made; dried; make it yourself; or only eat it in restaurants. Most of us I'm sure vary where we get our pasta fix from.

I like pasta because it is quick and easy, filling, and the range of sauces is only limited by the extent of your imagination. It is ideal dinner party food, and the filled pastas in particular can be frozen.

Most commercial pasta is made from durum wheat called semolina. However, fresh wholemeal flour will suffice.

If you don't wish to purchase a pasta machine I suggest you make homemade lasagne, tagliatelle or fettucine as this requires simply cutting the pasta dough with a sharp knife. As you become more adept at pasta making you may wish to make your own ravioli, tortellini, penne or cannelloni.

If the prospect of making home made pasta is too daunting, or you haven't got time, good quality wholemeal pastas are readily available. I hope you like the delicious quick and easy accompanying pasta sauces.

I am sure you have seen the red, green and yellow pasta in shops and restaurants. It is easy to colour homemade pasta using fresh vegetables and herbs. For example, if you want to make red coloured pasta add 2 tablespoons of tomato paste or puree per ½ kilogram of wholemeal flour. For green pasta squeeze the liquid from 1 cup of cooked fresh spinach. Add the colouring when you add the egg whites. Do not use artificial colourings. Red cabbage, capsicum, pumpkin, beetroot and many other vegetables and herbs can be used to colour pasta.

Pumpkin, Spinach & Ricotta Gnocchi

HOW TO MAKE PASTA AT HOME

500 grams wholemeal flour or semolina
4 egg whites
1 cup water

Sift the flour into a large bowl.
Make a well in the centre and pour in the egg whites
and water. Stir the mixture with a fork until the egg
white and flour is well combined.
Shape into a ball. If it seems to be a little dry sprinkle
on a little more water. Be careful though, not to make
the dough too sticky.
Knead the dough on a lightly floured board for
10 minutes until it is smooth.
Wrap the dough in a clean T-towel and leave
for 20 minutes.

The following method is for people who don't
have a pasta machine. However, this pasta dough can
be put through a pasta machine.

Making pasta is gratifying and lots of fun. The
first time I made pasta I was as delighted as when I
produced my first Christmas cake! Here we go...

1. Place the dough on a floured surface. Roll it out
using a rolling pin and roll into a paper thin rectangle.

2. Carefully transfer the pasta sheet onto a lightly
floured cloth. Leave it there for 45 minutes.

Now the fun begins. The big decision is what
shape pasta do you want. With a sharp knife cut the
pasta to the   shape you require.

Leave the cut pasta to stand for a few minutes,
and then its ready to plunge into your big cooking pot.

HOW TO COOK PASTA

You may think that heading is an insult to your
intelligence, but believe it or not pasta like rice is often
cooked incorrectly.

It is important you use a large saucepan or soup pot.
For 1 kilogram of pasta I recommend using a minimum
of 5 litres of water. Insufficient water causes
the pasta to congeal.

Wait until the water is boiling furiously, then drop
the pasta in. If you are using long strands of pasta –
spaghetti, fettucine, tagliatelle – bend the pasta
into the water, don't break it up.

HOW LONG SHOULD PASTA BE COOKED?

It is hard to estimate exactly how long to cook pasta. You MUST test it yourself to see when it is al dente – firm to the bite. The only thing worse than soggy pasta is cold pasta – that's supposed to be served hot!

Fresh pasta cooks quickly – 2-4 minutes; dried pasta 10-12 minutes, and filled pasta – ravioli, tortellini – 10 minutes.

There is a strange rumour going around that pasta should immediately be deluged with cold water once it has been cooked. Only do that if you wish to serve the pasta cold.

When I was a child my mother always spooned the bolognese sauce on top of our spaghetti. I think it is much better to mix the sauce in with the pasta before you serve it. If you pass the sauce around, by the time it has done the rounds, everyone's pasta will be cold.

HOW MUCH PASTA SHOULD BE SERVED?

As a general guide 100 grams of pasta per person is sufficient for a main course.

TOMATO SAUCE
Salsa di pomodoro

500 grams fresh ripe tomatoes roughly chopped
1 tablespoon tomato paste
3 cloves garlic finely chopped
1 medium onion finely sliced
1 cup water
freshly ground black pepper to taste

Place onion, garlic and water in saucepan.
Cover and simmer for 5 minutes.
Add all other ingredients. Cover and simmer
for 10 minutes. Puree in blender.
Serve with freshly cooked pasta.

Serves 4

TOMATO AND LEMON SAUCE
Salsa di pomodoro al limone

1 cup fresh lemon juice
500 grams fresh ripe tomatoes
1 tablespoon tomato paste
1 clove garlic
freshly ground black pepper to taste

Place all ingredients in saucepan and simmer covered
for 10 minutes. Puree in blender. Simmer for 5 minutes
and serve with freshly cooked pasta.

Serves 4

BOLOGNESE SAUCE
Salsa bolognese

400 grams lean minced veal
1 medium onion finely sliced
1 clove garlic finely chopped
1 tablespoon tomato paste
1 cup diced celery
1 medium carrot diced
1 tablespoon chopped fresh oregano, or
1 teaspoon dried oregano
1½ cups dry white wine
3 ripe medium tomatoes roughly chopped
1 cup water
freshly ground black pepper to taste

Place veal, water, garlic and onion in non stick
frypan. Simmer covered for 5 minutes.
Add to all other ingredients and simmer covered for 30
minutes. Serve with freshly cooked pasta.

Serves 4-6

GARLIC AND PARSLEY SAUCE
Salsa all'aglio e prezzemolo

Only true garlicaholics like me will appreciate
this addictive sauce.

10 cloves garlic finely chopped – yes 10!
1 cup finely chopped fresh parsley
1 cup unsweetened orange juice
freshly ground black pepper to taste

Blend all ingredients and mix through
freshly cooked pasta.

Serves 4

TUNA AND CELERY SAUCE
Salsa al tonno e sedano

1 - 425g tin tuna (water packed)
1 medium purple onion finely sliced
1 clove garlic finely chopped
3 ripe medium tomatoes roughly chopped
1 teaspoon finely chopped fresh sage or
½ teaspoon dried sage
2 cups diced celery
2 tablespoons finely chopped fresh parsley
1 cup water

Place water, onion, and garlic in non stick frypan.
Simmer covered for 5 minutes. Add all other
ingredients and simmer for 5 minutes.
This sauce is also delicious served cold uncooked
with cold pasta.

Serves 4-6

CHILLI SAUCE
Salsa al peperoncino

500 grams fresh ripe tomatoes
1 medium onion finely chopped
1 tablespoon tomato paste
2 fresh red or green chillies
½ cup water
freshly ground black pepper to taste

Place all ingredients in saucepan. Simmer covered for
10 minutes. Puree in blender and serve with freshly
cooked pasta.

Serves 4

TOMATO AND BASIL SAUCE
Salsa di pomodoro al basilico

1 cup water
3 cloves garlic
1 medium onion finely sliced
1 bunch fresh basil roughly chopped. Remove stalks
500 grams fresh ripe tomatoes
freshly ground black pepper to taste

Place onion, garlic and water in saucepan. Cover and
simmer for 5 minutes.
Add all other ingredients except basil, cover
and simmer for 10 minutes.
Puree in blender. Stir in basil and serve.

Serves 4

MUSHROOM AND RICOTTA SAUCE
Salsa de funghi e ricotta

300 grams fresh button mushrooms thinly sliced
2 cloves garlic finely chopped
300 grams fresh ricotta cheese
1 cup skim milk
freshly ground black pepper to taste

Garnish: Finely chopped fresh parsley.

Puree ricotta cheese with skim milk, garlic and black
pepper. Stir in sliced mushrooms. Garnish with parsley
and serve.

Serves 4

HEY PESTO SAUCE
Salsa al pesto

I think this sauce is the pesto de resistance! It is light,
zesty and 'different'. I hope you like it.

1 large bunch fresh basil. Remove stalks
Dried basil is NOT an option if you want the real thing
6 cloves garlic
1 cup pine nuts – optional
300 grams fresh ricotta cheese
¾ cup skim milk
freshly ground black pepper to taste

Mash all ingredients in a mortar and pestle or whizz in
the blender.
Mix through freshly cooked pasta.

Serves 4

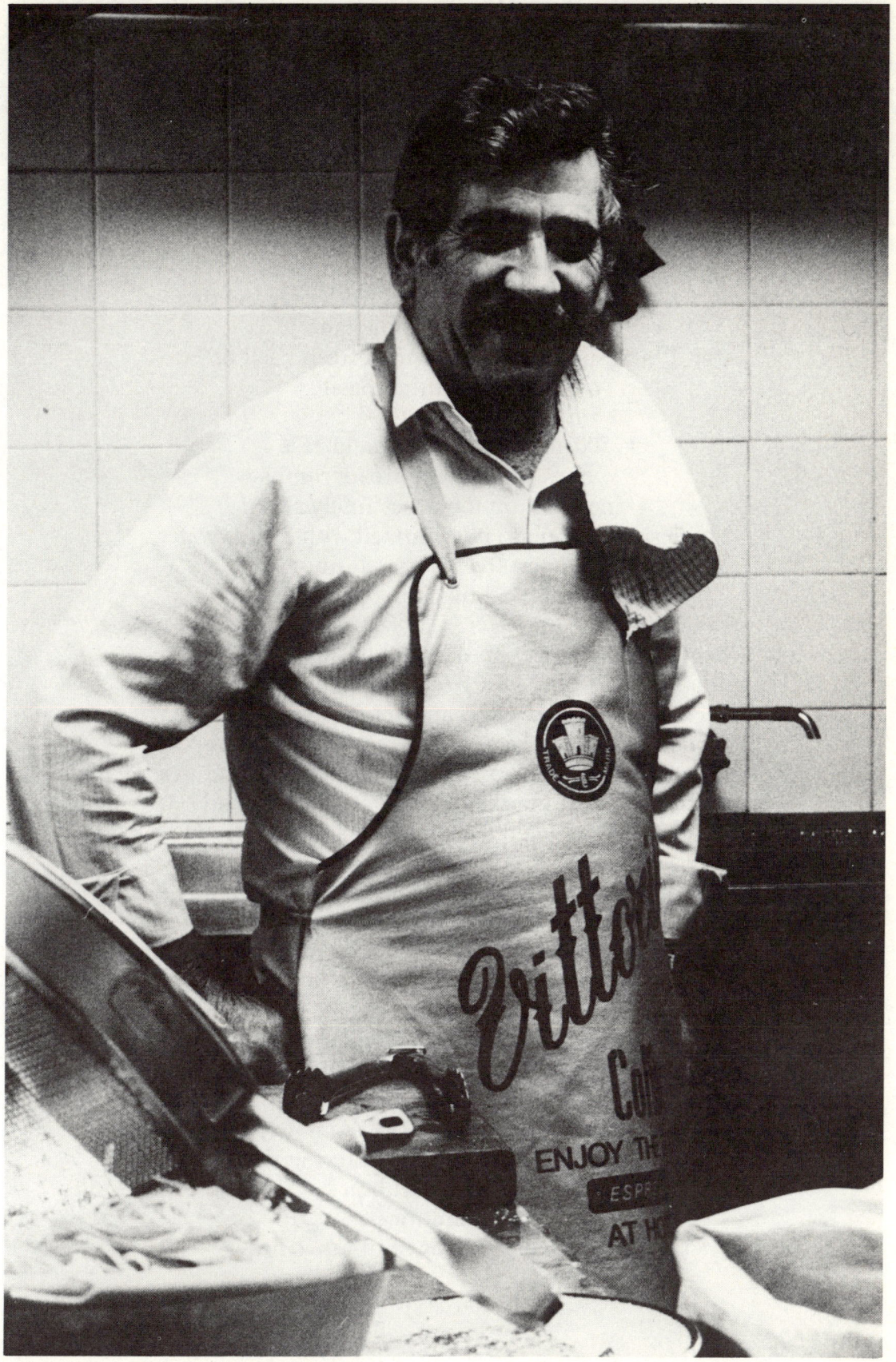

SPINACH LASAGNE
Lasagne agli spinaci

250 grams spinach lasagne sheets (about 12)
1 large bunch fresh spinach – trim off stalks
1 medium onion finely chopped
2 cloves garlic finely chopped
1 tablespoon finely chopped fresh oregano or
1 teaspoon dried oregano
1 tablespoon finely chopped fresh basil or
1 teaspoon dried basil
1 bay leaf
500 grams fresh ricotta cheese
2½ cups wholemeal breadcrumbs
4 ripe medium tomatoes finely sliced
2 tablespoons tomato paste mixed with 2 cups water
1 teaspoon freshly grated nutmeg
freshly ground black pepper to taste

Bring a large saucepan of water to the boil. Drop in spinach leaves, cover for 1 minute. Remove, drain well, finely chop and set aside.
Bring a large saucepan of water to the boil. Drop in lasagne sheets – 3 at a time. Cook for 10-12 minutes until tender. Plunge into cold water. Drain and set aside. (The pre-cooked lasagne sheets do not need to be boiled).
Mix ricotta cheese with breadcrumbs until mixture is crumbly.
Preheat oven to 200°C-400°F. Layer a non stick baking dish 30cmx20cm – about 12inx9in – in the following order:
4 lasagne sheets; portion of ricotta and breadcrumb mixture; spinach; tomatoes; onion and garlic; basil and oregano. Repeat the process three times. Top with last layer of lasagne sheets. Pour over tomato paste and water mixture. Sprinkle with remaining ricotta and breadcrumb mixture. Season with pepper and sprinkle with nutmeg.
Bake for 30-40 minutes until top is brown.

Serves 6

EASY PIZZA DOUGH

450 grams wholemeal self raising flour
125 grams fresh ricotta cheese
300 ml skim milk

Sift the flour. Tip bran husks back into the bowl. Rub
in the ricotta cheese until the mixture resembles
breadcrumbs. Slowly add the skim milk until a soft
dough is formed.
Place dough on floured board and knead for 5 minutes
until it is smooth and elastic. Allow to stand for 1 hour
wrapped in a clean T-towel. Using a lightly floured
rolling pin, roll out to required size and thickness. Roll
out to between 5mm-1cm (¼-½ inch) thick.
To cut out a round pizza, place a dinner plate on rolled
out dough, and slice around the edge with a sharp
knife. For mini pizzas cut around the rim of a drinking
glass. Place pizza base on pizza or non stick
baking tray.
Add topping of your choice and bake in a heated oven
200°C-400°F for 20-25 minutes. Serve hot or cold.
This quantity of dough makes 1 large pizza, 2 medium
or 6 mini pizzas.

If you are really in a hurry wholemeal pita bread
can serve as a pizza base.

PIZZA TOPPINGS WITH PIZAZZ

BASIC PIZZA TOMATO SAUCE
Pizza alla salsa di pomodoro

1 medium onion
2 cloves garlic
4 ripe medium tomatoes
1 tablespoon tomato paste
1 tablespoon finely chopped fresh oregano or
1 teaspoon dried oregano
1 tablespoon finely chopped fresh basil or
1 teaspoon dried basil
¼ cup water
1 teaspoon red wine vinegar
freshly ground black pepper to taste

Puree all ingredients in blender

VEGETARIAN SUPREME PIZZA TOPPING
Pizza suprema vegetariana

1 quantity basic tomato pizza sauce
1 cup fresh ricotta cheese
1 red or green capsicum cut into thin strips
1 cup finely sliced button mushrooms
1 zucchini finely sliced
1 tablespoon finely chopped fresh parsley

Spread uncooked pizza base with tomato sauce.
Add vegetables. Sprinkle with cheese and parsley and
bake at 200°C-400°F for 20 minutes.

SPINACH AND RICOTTA TOPPING
Coperta di spinaci e ricotta

250 grams fresh ricotta cheese
1 tablespoon skim milk
2 cups finely chopped fresh uncooked spinach
1 tablespoon finely chopped fresh parsley
1 teaspoon freshly grated nutmeg

Puree ricotta cheese with skim milk. Mix in chopped spinach and parsley. Spread onto uncooked pizza base. Sprinkle with nutmeg and bake at 200°C-400°F for 20 minutes

AUSSIE PIZZA TOPPING

2 cups cooked lean minced steak
5 egg whites cooked and chopped
1 medium white onion finely chopped
1 quantity basic pizza tomato sauce
2 tablespoons finely chopped fresh parsley

Spread tomato sauce onto uncooked pizza base.

Sprinkle with minced steak, egg whites, onions. Top with parsley. Bake at 200°C-400°F for 20 minutes.

MARINARA TOPPING
Coperta di condimento all a marinara

2 cups uncooked mixed seafood roughly chopped
(fish, prawns, calamari, scallops)
2 cloves garlic finely chopped
1 tablespoon finely chopped fresh oregano or
1 teaspoon dried oregano
1 quantity basic tomato pizza sauce
Freshly ground black pepper to taste

Spread tomato sauce on uncooked pizza base. Top with
mixed seafood. Sprinkle with oregano, season with
pepper and bake at 200°C-400°F for 20 minutes.

MUSHROOM AND BASIL TOPPING

250 grams button mushrooms finely sliced
½ bunch fresh basil finely chopped. Remove stalks
1 quantity basic pizza tomato sauce

Spread tomato sauce on uncooked pizza base.
Top with mushrooms and basil. Bake at
200°C-400°F for 20 minutes.

Easy Eggplant Bake

Mixed Italian Salad

Music fills this pastoral scene; the mood of quiet listening, the languid rhythm of a hot summer afternoon in the open air is implicit. Giorgione is known to have had a passion for music, and the lyrical atmosphere of this painting is consistent with his other works. The tranquil beauty of the nudes, the softened contours of their well-fleshed bodies, also mark them as creatures of Giorgione's romantic imagination. Their actions seem dreamlike and disengaged; the girl at the well pours water absentmindedly, the negligent flutist gazes not at her companion but into the distance.

There is a disturbing note here, however — a note of inconsistency. The young men are more solidly delineated by the painter's brush. They seem more animated and more individualized than are Giorgione's usual subjects. Even the landscape is unlike his active, integrated natural settings.

Here is the heart of the matter, the center of a controversy that has plagued art historians: who painted this picture? Even the title, given here in French because the picture is owned by the Louvre, is disputed. Known widely as *Fête Champêtre*, or "Country Feast," the picture has had many other names, including "Pastoral Symphony" and "Fountain of Love." The answer to the question may never be found, but in the analysis of style related above lies a most persuasive explanation: Giorgione selected the theme and perhaps painted the women and certain other details; Titian painted the men, much of the landscape and perhaps was responsible for integrating the entire work. It would seem that both men worked on the painting, perhaps even at the same time.

Giorgione and Titian *Fête Champêtre*, c.15..

72

73

Broccoli Bologna

VEGETABLES, SALADS, RICE & POLENTA

Italian vegetables and salads are fantastic.

I will never forget going to the markets in Florence early in the morning, and seeing the myriad range of crisp fruit and vegetables.

Be adventurous! If you haven't tried fennel, radicchio, or artichokes your taste buds are in for a pleasant surprise.

Veal Bianco

HERBED POTATO CROQUETTES
Crocchette di patate alle erbe

1 kg potatoes peeled, boiled and mashed
2 cloves garlic finely chopped
3 egg whites
100 grams fresh ricotta cheese
2 cups wholemeal breadcrumbs
1 tablespoon finely chopped fresh oregano or
1 teaspoon dried oregano
1 tablespoon finely chopped fresh basil or
1 teaspoon dried basil
freshly ground black pepper to taste

Combine mashed potato, garlic, ricotta cheese, herbs
and pepper. Lightly beat egg whites and set aside.
Roll mixture into small balls. Dip into egg white and
firmly coat with breadcrumbs.
Preheat oven to 200°C-400°F. Bake for
30 minutes until brown

Serves 4-6

SPINACH AND RICOTTA GNOCCHI

Gnocchi di spinaci e ricotta

1 medium bunch fresh spinach
300 grams fresh ricotta cheese
1 egg white
1 tablespoon wholemeal breadcrumbs
1 teaspoon freshly grated nutmeg
freshly ground black pepper to taste
1 cup wholemeal flour

Wash spinach well and discard stalks.
Steam spinach for 2 minutes and chop finely.
Drain off all excess liquid.
Mix with ricotta cheese, egg white, breadcrumbs,
nutmeg and pepper.
Form this mixture into small balls and roll lightly in
wholemeal flour. Bring a large saucepan of water to the
boil. Drop in 4 gnocchi at a time. Reduce heat and
simmer for 3 minutes. Remove with a slotted spoon.
Gnocchi can be served by itself or with a pasta
sauce of your choice.

EASY EGGPLANT BAKE
Melanzane al forno semplici

3 medium eggplants
2 tablespoons finely chopped fresh oregano or
2 teaspoons dried oregano
4 ripe medium tomatoes
1 cup dry white wine
1 tablespoon tomato paste
freshly ground black pepper to taste
300 grams fresh ricotta cheese
1½ cups wholemeal breadcrumbs

Rub ricotta cheese into breadcrumbs until mixture is
crumbly and set aside.
Slice eggplants into thin discs. Place onto kitchen paper
for 5 minutes to absorb bitter juices. In non stick round
or square baking dish layer eggplant slices, tomato
slices and herbs. Top with a layer of eggplant slices.
Mix tomato paste with white wine and pour over.
Season with pepper. Top with ricotta
and breadcrumb mixture.
Preheat oven to 200°C-400°F.
Bake for 40 minutes and serve.

Serves 4-6

SAVOURY BEAN CREPES

Frittelle saporite di fagioli

CREPE BATTER:

1 cup wholemeal flour
2 cups skim milk
4 egg whites stiffly beaten

Add flour to milk and stir until well combined.
Fold in egg whites. Place crepe batter in refrigerator
for 2 hours.
To make crepes, heat a non stick frypan. Pour in small
quantity of batter. Swirl around pan base until batter is
evenly distributed. Cook 2 minutes on each side.
Set aside.

FILLING:

2 x 310 gram tins of borlotti or cannellini beans. Rinse
with cold water to remove excess salt, and drain.

500 grams fresh button mushrooms finely sliced
1 ripe medium tomato finely sliced
2 tablespoons finely chopped fresh oregano or
2 teaspoons dried oregano
freshly ground black pepper to taste

Place filling ingredients in saucepan. Simmer and stir
for 5 minutes until heated through. Allow to cool. Blend
or mash. Spread mixture onto crepes. Roll up into a
tube shape. Preheat oven to 200°C-400°F. Place crepes
on non stick baking tray and heat through for 10
minutes. Serve immediately.

Makes 6 crepes

STUFFED TOMATOES
Pomidoro ripieni

8 ripe medium tomatoes
1 medium onion finely chopped
½ green or red capsicum finely chopped
¼ cup water
2 cups cooked brown rice
1 clove garlic finely chopped
1 tablespoon finely chopped fresh basil or
1 teaspoon dried basil
1 tablespoon finely chopped fresh parsley
250 grams fresh ricotta cheese

Slice the top off each tomato. Set aside tops.
Scoop out tomato flesh and chop. Simmer onion and
garlic in water for 5 minutes. Combine all ingredients
and mix well. Drain off excess liquid. Spoon mixture
back into tomato cases. Place tomato tops back and put
on non stick baking tray. Bake in preheated oven
180°C-350°F for 15 minutes and serve.

Serves 4-6

CARROTS IN RICOTTA SAUCE
Carote alla salsa di ricotta

10 medium carrots washed, peeled and finely sliced
250 grams fresh ricotta cheese
1 cup skim milk
1 tablespoon finely chopped fresh parsley

Steam carrots for 5 minutes.
Blend ricotta cheese with skim milk and pour
over hot carrots.
Garnish with parsley and serve.

Serves 4-6

MYRTLEFORD MUSHROOMS
Funghi ripieni

1 was brought up in North Eastern Victoria near
Beechworth. Myrtleford is a neighbouring town with a
large Italian population. The area is renowned for
its delicious field mushrooms which inspired
this zesty dish.

16 medium mushrooms
1 medium onion finely chopped
2 cloves garlic finely chopped
2 tablespoons finely chopped fresh parsley
125 grams fresh ricotta cheese
2 cups wholemeal breadcrumbs
freshly ground black pepper to taste

Cut off mushroom stalks and finely chop. In non stick
frypan stir fry mushroom stalks, onion and garlic for 3
minutes. Remove from frypan. Mix with ricotta cheese,
breadcrumbs, pepper and parsley.
Stuff the mixture into mushroom caps. Place
mushrooms capside down on non stick baking tray. Pre
heat oven to 200°C-400°F and bake for 20 minutes.

Serves 4-6

VEGETABLES VENEZIA
Verdure all veneziana

1 clove garlic
¼ red cabbage
1 zucchini
2 carrots
1 red capsicum
1 medium onion
1 medium tomato
1 cup red or white wine vinegar
1 cup unsweetened orange juice
freshly ground black pepper to taste

Finely slice all vegetables and season with pepper.
Marinate in refrigerator for 24 hours and serve

Serves 4-6

BERTOLUCCI BEANS
Fagioli bertolucci

Bertolucci is the famous Italian film director.
Remember 'that' film 'Last Tango in Paris'?

1 x 310 gram tin borlotti or cannellini beans.
Or 250 grams of the dried variety.
(Soak in cold water overnight,
or in boiling water for 2 hours before use.)
2 cloves garlic finely chopped
2 medium onions finely sliced
2 ripe medium tomatoes roughly chopped
1 tablespoon tomato paste
1 tablespoon fresh sage or
1 teaspoon dried sage
1 cup vegetable stock
freshly ground black pepper to taste

Wash beans in colander to remove salt.
Place garlic and onion in large saucepan with stock.
Simmer covered for 5 minutes. Add all other
ingredients and simmer covered for 15 minutes.

Serves 4-6

BABY SQUASH WITH HERBS
Zuccarelle Tenere alle erbe

1 kg mixed yellow and green baby squash

1 bay leaf

2 cloves garlic chopped

2 tablespoons finely chopped fresh parsley

Bring a large saucepan of water to the boil Add garlic
and bay leaf. Plunge in squash and cook for 5 minutes.
Drain in colander and serve garnished
with chopped parsley.

Serves 4-6

BROCCOLI BOLOGNA

Broccoli alla bolognese

1 head of fresh broccoli
4 cloves garlic finely chopped
½ cup toasted pine nuts – optional
2 tablespoons finely chopped fresh parsley

Trim broccoli and cut into flowerets
Place garlic in large saucepan of water and steam
broccoli for 5 minutes. Remove from steamer. Sprinkle
with pine nuts and parsley and serve.

Serves 4-6

STUFFED BUTTERNUT PUMPKIN
Noce di burro bella

1 medium butternut pumpkin
2 cloves garlic finely chopped
1 medium onion finely chopped
¾ cup water
1 cup cooked brown rice
2 ripe medium tomatoes roughly chopped
1 tablespoon finely chopped fresh oregano or
1 teaspoon dried oregano
1 tablespoon red wine vinegar
freshly ground black pepper to taste

Simmer the onion and garlic in water in covered non
stick frypan for 5 minutes. Add all other ingredients
and simmer for 5 minutes.
Drain off excess liquid
Cut the pumpkin in half lengthwise and scoop out
seeds. If the pumpkin cavity is small scrape out some of
the pumpkin flesh. Stuff mixture into the halves. Cover
with foil and bake at 200°C-400°F for 25 minutes.
Remove foil and bake for 5 minutes.

Serves 4-6

STUFFED ZUCCHINI
Zucchini ripeni

8 medium size zucchini
1 small onion finely chopped
1 clove garlic finely chopped
250 grams fresh ricotta cheese
1 cup wholemeal breadcrumbs
1 tablespoon finely chopped fresh oregano or
1 teaspoon dried oregano

Bring a large saucepan of water to the boil.
Plunge zucchini in for 2 minutes and drain in colander.
Cut in half lengthways and scoop out flesh. Set aside.
Mix breadcrumbs, oregano, garlic, onion and ricotta
cheese until mixture is crumbly. Mix in zucchini flesh.
Stuff mixture back into zucchini shells. Preheat oven to
200°C-400°F and bake for 20 minutes.

Serves 4

ARTICHOKES

Globe artichokes are revered in Italy – understandably – they are an outstanding vegetable. Don't be put off by their 'awkward' appearance. They are delicious, easy to prepare and can be cooked many ways – baked, boiled, steamed, stuffed, braised etc.

HOW TO PREPARE ARTICHOKES

Snap off the tough woody external leaves, so that only the white, tender part of the leaf is left. Keep removing the darker leaves until a flower like core of young leaves can be seen.

Cut off about 25mm – 1 inch – off the top of the artichoke. Sprinkle with lemon juice. Then remove the little inner leaves and the fuzz or choke beneath them. Cut off a large proportion of the stem, and trim away the outer layer until the white core is visible. Remember to squeeze lemon juice over all the cut parts as this prevents discolouration.

This flavoursome dish is easy to cook and tasty!

ROMAN ARTICHOKES
Carciofi alla romana

8 medium globe artichokes
3 cloves garlic finely chopped
1 cup finely chopped parsley
1 cup fresh lemon juice
1 cup dry white wine
½ cup water
2 cups wholemeal breadcrumbs
freshly ground black pepper to taste

Prepare the artichokes as described above.
Combine garlic, parsley, lemon juice and breadcrumbs.
Stuff the mixture into the tops of the artichokes.
Season with pepper.
Place artichokes in non stick baking dish.
Pour over wine and water.
Preheat oven to 180°C-375°F and bake for 30 minutes.

Serves 4-6

PUMPKIN GNOCCHI
Gnocchi di zucca

1kg pumpkin
1 egg white
300 grams wholemeal breadcrumbs
3 cloves garlic finely chopped
1 tablespoon finely chopped fresh parsley
1 teaspoon freshly grated nutmeg
freshly ground black pepper to taste
1 bay leaf
1 cup wholemeal flour

Peel the pumpkin and steam until tender
– about 15 minutes
Mash pumpkin with egg white, breadcrumbs, parsley,
garlic, nutmeg and pepper.
Take small quantities of mixture and roll into marble
size balls. Lightly roll in wholemeal flour. Bring a large
saucepan of water to the boil, with the bay leaf. Drop in
6 gnocchi at a time. Reduce heat and simmer for 3-4
minutes. Remove with a slotted spoon. Drain on
kitchen paper and serve with your favourite pasta
sauce.

Serves 6

Siesta Seafood Salad

Pisa Peaches

Figaro Cake

EGGPLANTS ROMA
Melanzane alla romana

3 medium eggplants cut lengthwise
2 medium onions finely chopped
300 grams lean minced steak
¼ cup water
2 cloves garlic finely chopped
2 ripe medium tomatoes roughly chopped
1 tablespoon tomato paste
1 egg white
1 tablespoon fresh oregano finely chopped or
1 teaspoon dried oregano
500 grams fresh ricotta cheese
2 cups wholemeal breadcrumbs
freshly ground black pepper to taste

Place eggplant halves face down on kitchen paper for 5 minutes to absorb bitter juices. Scoop out eggplant flesh and set aside. In non stick frypan simmer covered with water, onions, garlic, eggplant flesh, and tomatoes for 5 minutes. Add minced steak and stir fry for 5 minutes. Stir in oregano, pepper, tomato paste and egg white. Drain off excess liquid. Spoon mixture back into eggplant shells. Mix ricotta cheese with breadcrumbs until mixture is crumbly. Sprinkle mixture on top of eggplants. Preheat oven to 200°C-400°F. Bake for 30 minutes.

Serves 6

Fresh Fruit Gelato

VEGETARIAN RISOTTO
Risotto vegetariano

For a variation the mushrooms can be substituted with
125 grams skinned, diced, uncooked chicken breasts.
The vegetable stock can also be substituted with
defatted chicken or beef stock.

500 grams uncooked brown rice
1 medium onion finely chopped
1 clove garlic finely chopped
3 zucchini finely sliced
1 red pepper diced
125 grams button mushrooms finely sliced
2 cups par boiled green peas
1 medium carrot diced
1 litre vegetable stock
1 cup water
1 pinch saffron

Simmer all ingredients except rice, saffron and stock in
covered non stick saucepan for 5 minutes.
Drain off excess liquid.
Bring stock to the boil. Add rice and cook for 20
minutes. Add remaining ingredients, and stir in saffron.
Simmer for 10 minutes until all stock is absorbed.

Serves 6

POLENTA

POLENTA is a delicious accompaniment to spicy
dishes, and is especially popular in Northern Italy.
If possible, try to purchase coursely ground cornmeal.
For an even better flavour grind your own cornmeal.

1 litre water
250 grams coursely ground cornmeal

Place the water in a large saucepan and bring to the
boil. Reduce heat to simmering. Slowly add the
cornmeal, and continue stirring until mixture is
thick. Simmer uncovered over a moderate heat for
15-20 minutes. Stir frequently. Turn polenta onto
plate or chopping board. Wet the back of a spoon
and mould into required shape and size.
Allow to cool. Cut into slices and serve.

Serves 6

TEMPTING TUNA SALAD
Insalata di tonno

1 x 425 gram tin tuna (water packed)
150 grams tinned cannellini
or borlotti beans
1 medium purple onion thinly sliced
½ cup red wine vinegar
1 tablespoon finely chopped fresh parsley
freshly ground black pepper to taste

Rinse beans in cold water to remove excess salt.
Combine all ingredients and serve.

Serves 4-6

MIXED ITALIAN SALAD
Insalata mista Italiana

Whenever I am tossing an Italian mixed salad I
remember the wonderful summer I spent on the Italian
Riviera. Grilled fresh fish and a crisp salad was a
standing order for lunch.

1 radicchio
2 crisp mignonette lettuces
1 green pepper finely sliced
1 red pepper finely sliced
2 ripe medium tomatoes sliced
½ cucumber finely sliced
1 clove garlic finely chopped
8 radishes finely sliced

DRESSING:
1 cup unsweetened orange juice
Squeeze of fresh lemon juice
1 tablespoon red or white wine vinegar
1 tablespoon finely chopped fresh parsley
freshly ground black pepper to taste

Rinse, drain and tear up lettuce leaves and radicchio. Add all other
ingredients. Let dressing marinate in refrigerator for 30
minutes. Pour over dressing just before serving.

Serves 4-6

CAPRI CARROT SALAD

Insalata di carote alla capri

6 medium carrots
1 purple onion
1 tablespoon finely chopped fresh parsley
½ cup fresh lemon juice

Peel and grate carrots
Peel and finely dice onion
Combine all ingredients and serve

FENNEL SALAD
Insalata di finocchi

2 large fennel bulbs
1 cucumber finely sliced
1 red capsicum finely sliced
1 small onion finely sliced

DRESSING:
3 tablespoons unsweetened orange juice
1 tablespoon red or white wine vinegar
1 tablespoon chopped fresh mint
freshly ground black pepper to taste

Remove outer leaves from fennel bulbs and finely slice.
Mix with other salad vegetables. Marinate dressing in
refrigerator for 30 minutes. Pour over dressing just
before serving.

Serves 4-6

CAULIFLOWER SALAD
Insalata di cavolfiore

1 medium cauliflower
1 bay leaf
1 cup red wine vinegar
1 tablespoon finely chopped fresh parsley

Wash and trim cauliflower of leaves
Bring a large saucepan of water to the boil
Immerse bay leaf, and plunge in cauliflower.
Reduce heat and simmer for 10 minutes. Drain and
allow to cool. Slice into small flowerets, drench with
vinegar and sprinkle with parsley.

Serves 4-6

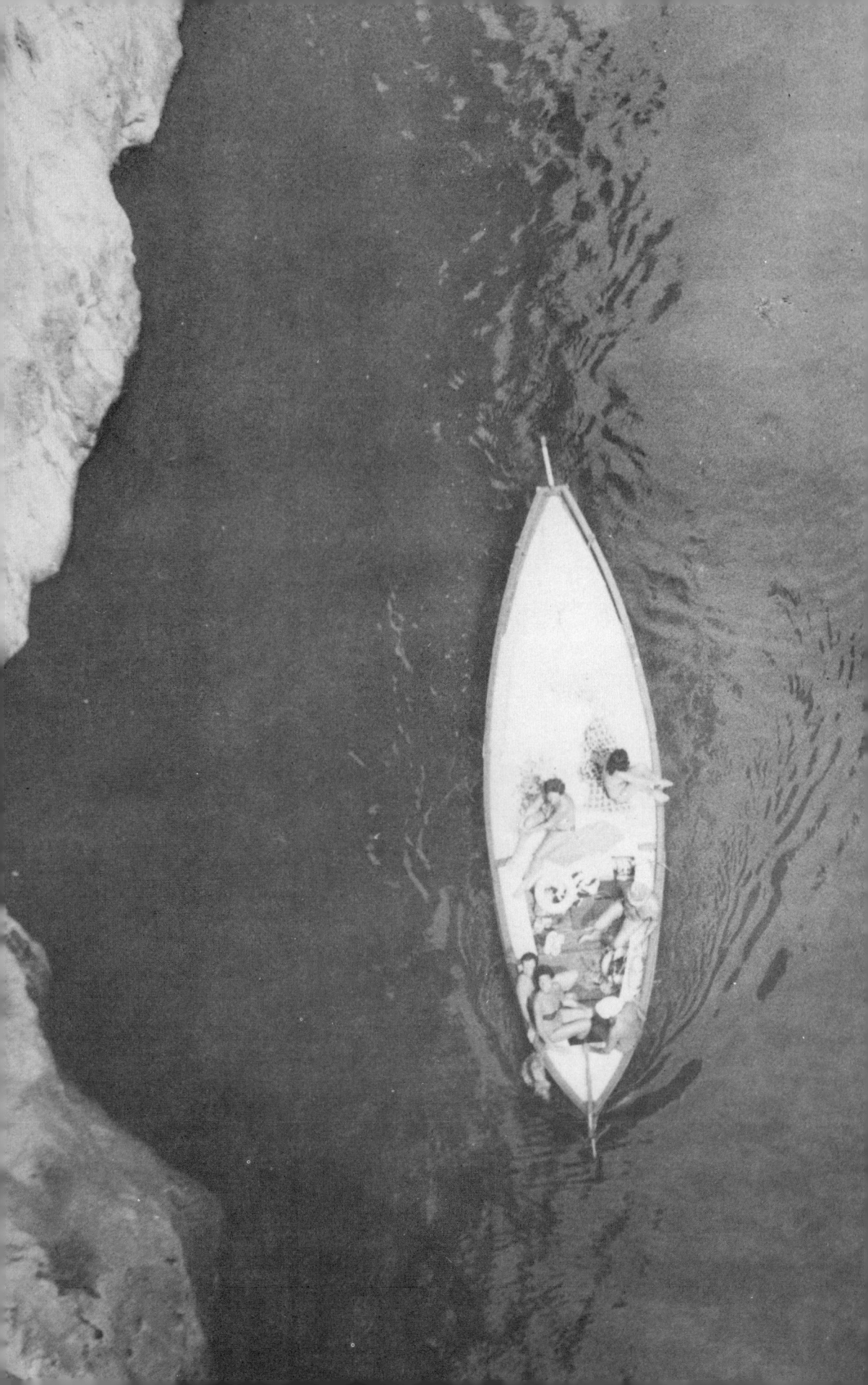

SEAFOOD

The taste of Italian seafood is sensational.
What appeals to me most about Italian fish dishes is that they really are quick and easy to prepare.

Grilling, dry frying at a high temperature or baking is the best way to prepare fish Italian style.

Serve the following recipes with a crisp salad, your favourite vegetable dishes, rice or polenta.

And, if you are interested in having the holiday of a lifetime, the Italian Riviera – with its kilometres of EXCELLENT seafood restaurants is a must!

SIESTA SEAFOOD SALAD
Insalata di frutti de mare

After this delicious, but filling salad you will probably
feel like a siesta!

225 grams fresh cooked prawns
225 grams calamari – washed and cleaned
225 grams scallops washed and trimmed
¼ cup red or white wine vinegar
3 medium carrots peeled and thinly sliced
2 medium purple onions finely sliced
1 red capsicum thinly sliced
2 cloves garlic finely sliced
1 teaspoon fresh sage chopped or
½ teaspoon dried sage
1 cup fresh lemon juice
freshly ground black pepper to taste

GARNISH: Fresh parsley finely chopped

Cut the calamari into 5mm (¼ inch rings)
Bring a large saucepan of water to the boil. Plunge
calamari in. Reduce heat and simmer for 10 minutes.
Set aside. Re-boil water and plunge in scallops.
Simmer for 5 minutes. Allow seafood to cool. Combine
well with all other ingredients. Marinate for 1 hour
in refrigerator, garnish and serve.

Serves 4-6

GARLIC PRAWNS
Gamberi all'aglio

300 grams fresh shelled, uncooked, deveined prawns
6 cloves garlic finely chopped
1 tablespoon finely chopped fresh parsley
½ cup fresh lemon juice
freshly ground black pepper to taste

GARNISH: Lemon wedges

Combine all ingredients and marinate for 1 hour.
Drain off lemon juice. Make sure prawns are
still coated with garlic and parsley.
Preheat griller to high. Grill prawns for
3 minutes on each side.
Garnish with lemon wedges and serve.

Serves 4-6

GENOA GRILLED FISH
Pesce alla griglia

1 whole fish – snapper, whiting, perch
cleaned and scaled
1 cup lemon juice
½ cup white wine vinegar
1 clove garlic finely chopped
2 sprigs fresh rosemary
2 bay leaves
2 cups wholemeal breadcrumbs

GARNISH: Lemon wedges

Combine all ingredients. Marinate fish in all
ingredients for 2 hours. Preheat griller to high.
Grill for 10 minutes on each side, or until
fish flesh is white when flaked with a fork.
Garnish with lemon wedges and serve.

Serves 4

FISH FEAST
Banchetto di pesce

This hearty fish stew is great for a dinner party
served with risotto.

1kg assorted, uncooked, cleaned fish
Add in a few uncooked prawns and pieces of calamari
(optional)
1 bay leaf
2 cups dry white wine
2 medium onions roughly chopped
3 ripe medium tomatoes roughly chopped
½ cup finely chopped fresh parsley
freshly ground black pepper to taste

Cut fish into small chunks, and roughly slice prawns
and calamari. Combine all ingredients except parsley.
Simmer for 40 minutes. Remove bay leaf. Sprinkle
with parsley and serve.

Serves 4-6

COLD MARINATED FISH
Pesce freddo marinato

700 grams whiting fillets
cut into small chunks
1 tablespoon red wine vinegar
3 cloves garlic finely chopped
1 tablespoon finely chopped fresh oregano or
1 teaspoon dried oregano
½ cup fresh lemon juice
½ cup unsweetened orange juice
freshly ground black pepper to taste
1½ cups water

Place water in non stick frypan and bring to the boil.
Add fish chunks and simmer covered for 10 minutes.
Remove from frypan and drain. Add to all other
ingredients. Marinate overnight and serve cold.

Serves 4-6

SICILIAN SARDINES
Sardine siciliane

If your only memories of sardines are the pungent
odours emanating from the tired sandwiches in
your school lunchbox, this succulent seafood
dish will inspire you.

12 fresh sardines scaled and cleaned
4 egg whites
2 cups wholemeal flour
4 cloves garlic finely chopped
2 cups fresh lemon juice

GARNISH: Lemon wedges and finely chopped
fresh parsley

Marinate sardines in garlic and lemon juice for 1 hour
before cooking. Remove from marinade and drain. Dip
sardines in flour then egg white. Dry fry in non stick
frypan – 5 minutes each side.
Garnish with lemon wedges and parsley.

Serves 4-6

P.S. Sardines are not recommended for people on the
Pritikin Regression eating plan.

POULTRY

Poultry cooked with fresh herbs is what makes Italian chicken and turkey dishes distinctive.

The fattier birds – pheasant, goose, and duck are not represented here.

Most of these dishes are delicious served either hot or cold. Roast rosemary chicken is fantastic for a picnic.

ROAST ROSEMARY CHICKEN
Pollo arrosto al rosmarino

This superb aromatic dish is tasty served hot or cold

1 medium chicken with all skin and
visible fat removed
6 cloves garlic finely chopped
freshly grated rind of 1 lemon
1 cup fresh lemon juice
3 tablespoons fresh rosemary finely chopped
or 3 teaspoons dried rosemary
freshly ground black pepper to taste

In a non stick frypan quickly brown chicken at a high
temperature on all sides.
Remove and place in deep non stick baking dish.
Combine all ingredients. Paste half the mixture on
outside of the bird, and the remainder in the cavity.
Cover with foil and roast in a preheated oven at 190°C-
375°F for 40 minutes. Baste occasionally during
cooking. Remove foil for last 10 minutes of
cooking to crisp the chicken.

Serves 4-6

SPICY BARBECUED CHICKEN
Pollo piccante alla graticola

Australians and Italians enjoy outdoor eating. This
dish is ideal for summer barbecues. If it rains, it can be
grilled!

4 chicken breasts with all skin removed
4 garlic cloves finely chopped
2 fresh red or green chillies finely chopped
1 cup fresh lemon juice
freshly ground black pepper to taste

Slash the chicken breasts with a sharp knife.
Combine remaining ingredients and marinate chicken
overnight.
Preheat barbecue and cook chicken breasts for 5
minutes on each side.

Serves 4

PEASANT CHICKEN CASSEROLE
Pollo alla paesana in casseruola

1 medium chicken with all skin and
visible fat removed. Cut into 6 pieces
4 cups defatted chicken or vegetable stock
2 medium onions finely sliced
2 cloves garlic finely chopped
250 grams button mushrooms sliced
1 bay leaf
2 sprigs fresh thyme
1 tablespoon cornflour
Freshly ground black pepper to taste

GARNISH: Finely chopped fresh parsley

Place all ingredients except garnish in large saucepan
and simmer for 40 minutes.
Remove bay leaf, garnish and serve.

Serves 4-6

MILANO CHICKEN
Pollo alla milanese

4 medium chicken breasts with all skin
and visible fat removed
2 cloves garlic finely chopped
1 cup dry white wine
½ cup water
½ cup unsweetened orange juice
1 tablespoon chopped fresh sage or
1 teaspoon dried sage
2 tablespoons cornflour mixed with
2 tablespoons cold water
Squeeze of lemon juice

GARNISH: Finely chopped fresh parsley

Place water, garlic and chicken breasts in non stick
frypan. Simmer for 5 minutes. Add all ingredients
except garnish and simmer for 10 minutes. Stir
in cornflour mixture and simmer for 3-4 minutes.
Garnish with parsley and serve.

Serves 4-6

MARSALA TURKEY BREASTS
Petti di tacchino al marsala

500 grams turkey breasts with all skin
and visible fat removed.
250 grams button mushrooms thinly sliced
1 tablespoon lemon juice
2 sprigs fresh rosemary or
1 teaspoon dried rosemary
½ cup marsala
1 cup defatted chicken stock
½ cup wholemeal flour
freshly ground black pepper to taste

GARNISH: Lemon wedges

Slice turkey breasts into thin strips.
Lightly coat with wholemeal flour.
Preheat a non stick frypan and fry strips on
both sides for 3 minutes. Add the stock to the
frypan and stir fry mushrooms for 2 minutes.
Add lemon juice, marsala and rosemary.
Simmer and stir for 3-5 minutes.
Garnish with lemon wedges and serve.

Serves 4

CHICKEN CACCIATORE
Pollo alla cacciatora

1 medium chicken with all skin
and visible fat removed. Cut into 6 pieces
1 medium onion finely sliced
3 cloves garlic finely chopped
1½ cups dry white wine
4 ripe medium tomatoes roughly chopped
1 tablespoon tomato paste
1 bay leaf
freshly ground black pepper to taste

GARNISH: Finely chopped fresh parsley

Place all ingredients except parsley in large saucepan.
Cover and simmer for 40 minutes until tender. Gravy
can be thickened with a little cornflour. Remove
bay leaf. Garnish and serve.

Serves 4-6

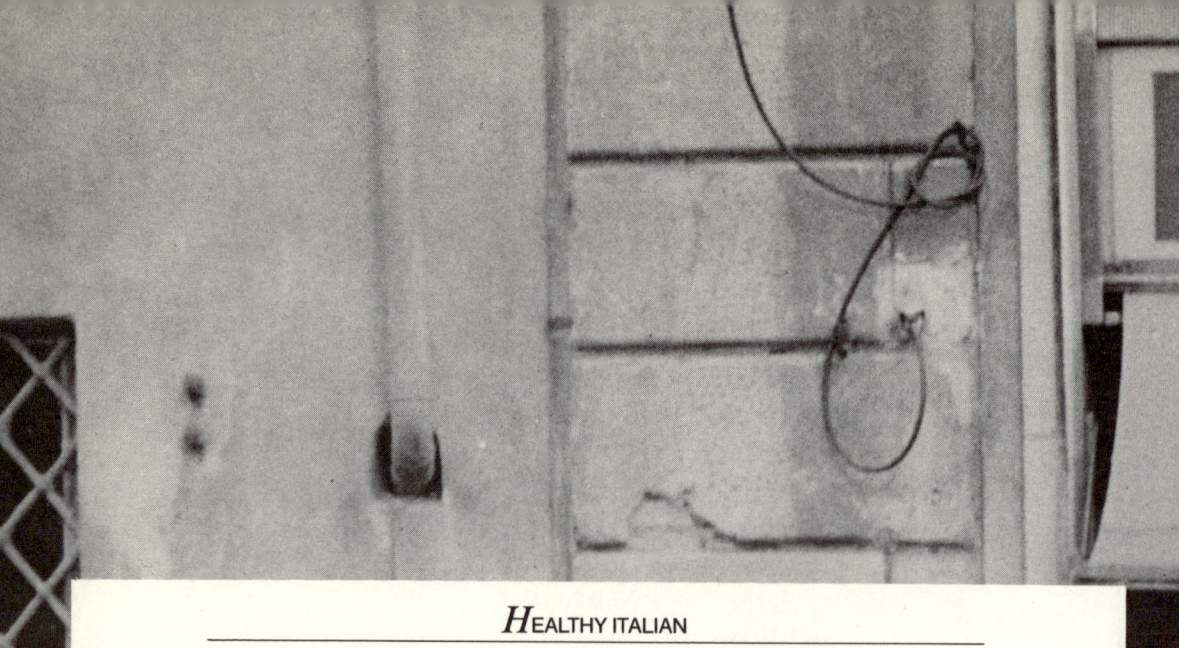

MEAT

I have included beef and veal recipes in this section.
If you enjoy lamb, lean tender cuts can be used. Any of the sauces or marinades for beef and veal can be used for lamb.

When you are preparing meat make sure you remove all visible fat before cooking.

OSSO BUCO
Osso buco

4 thick slices of shin of veal – osso buco
1 cup wholemeal flour
2 cloves garlic finely chopped
1 medium onion finely sliced
3 ripe medium tomatoes roughly chopped
2 small carrots finely sliced
1 cup dry white wine
1½ cups defatted vegetable or beef stock
Finely grated rind of 1 lemon
1 cup finely chopped fresh parsley
freshly ground black pepper to taste

Place 1 cup stock in non stick frypan with garlic and
onion. Simmer covered for 5 minutes.
Lightly coat the veal in flour, season with pepper and
add to the frypan. Fry for 5 minutes on either side.
Add the tomatoes, carrots, wine and remaining stock.
Cover and simmer for 1 hour. Sprinkle with lemon rind
and fresh parsley and simmer for 5 minutes.

Serves 4-6

BEEF IN RED WINE
Manzo al vino rosso

600 grams lean beef trimmed of all visible fat
250 grams button mushrooms finely sliced
1 medium onion finely sliced
2 tablespoons tomato paste
1 bay leaf
5 medium zucchini finely sliced
2 cloves garlic finely chopped
1½ cups red wine
1½ cups water
1 teaspoon finely chopped fresh marjoram or
½ teaspoon dried marjoram
1 tablespoon cornflour mixed with
2 tablespoons cold water
freshly ground black pepper to taste

Cube the beef. Place in non stick frypan and
sear on all sides.
Put all ingredients except cornflour in large saucepan.
Cover and simmer for 1 hour. Stir in cornflour mixture.
Simmer for 5 minutes. Remove bay leaf and serve.

Serves 4-6

MEDITERRANEAN MEATBALLS
Polpette all mediterranea

600 grams lean minced steak
1 medium onion finely diced
2 medium potatoes peeled boiled and mashed
1 egg white
2 cloves garlic finely chopped
2 tablespoons finely chopped fresh oregano or
2 teaspoons dried oregano
½ cup finely diced celery
1 cup wholemeal breadcrumbs
1 cup wholemeal flour

SAUCE:
4 ripe medium tomatoes pureed in blender
2 tablespoons tomato paste
¼ cup red or white wine vinegar
2 cups unsweetened apple juice
1 tablespoon cornflour mixed with
2 tablespoons cold water
freshly ground black pepper to taste

GARNISH: Finely chopped fresh parsley

Combine all meatball ingredients except flour. Roll
into small meatballs. Lightly roll in flour and brown on
all sides in non stick frypan – 15 minutes.
Mix together sauce ingredients and pour over
meatballs. Simmer covered for 15 minutes. Garnish
with parsley and serve.

Serves 8

VEAL BIANCO
Vitello al vino bianco

6 small veal steaks with all visible fat removed
125 grams button mushrooms thinly sliced
1 medium onion thinly sliced
1 clove garlic finely chopped – optional
1 cup dry sherry or white wine
¼ cup water
250 grams fresh ricotta cheese
½ cup skim milk
1 tablespoon cornflour mixed with
2 tablespoons cold water
freshly ground black pepper to taste

Puree skim milk with ricotta cheese and set aside.
Flatten veal steaks until thin. In non stick frypan cover
and simmer onion and garlic in water for 5 minutes.
Add veal and cook for 2 minutes on each side. Add
sherry, cornflour mixture, mushrooms and pepper.
Simmer and stir for 4 minutes. Pour in ricotta cheese
and skim milk puree. Simmer for 1 minute and serve.

Serves 6

SALTIMBOCCA
Saltimbocca

8 thin veal steaks
8 sage leaves or
1 teaspoon dried sage
1½ cups dry white wine
1 cup wholemeal flour
freshly ground black pepper to taste

Place a sage leaf or sprinkling of sage on each veal
steak. Fold over and secure each steak with a toothpick.
Roll lightly in wholemeal flour. Heat a non stick frypan
and dry fry on both sides for 5 minutes. Add wine,
and simmer and stir for 5 minutes.
Season with pepper and serve.

Serves 6

MARINATED STEAK
Bistecca marinata

4 small fillet steaks
4 teaspoons black peppercorns crushed
4 cloves garlic finely chopped
2 cups red wine

Combine all ingredients and marinate overnight. Drain
steak from marinade. Preheat griller to high. Cook
steak on either side until tender.

Serves 4

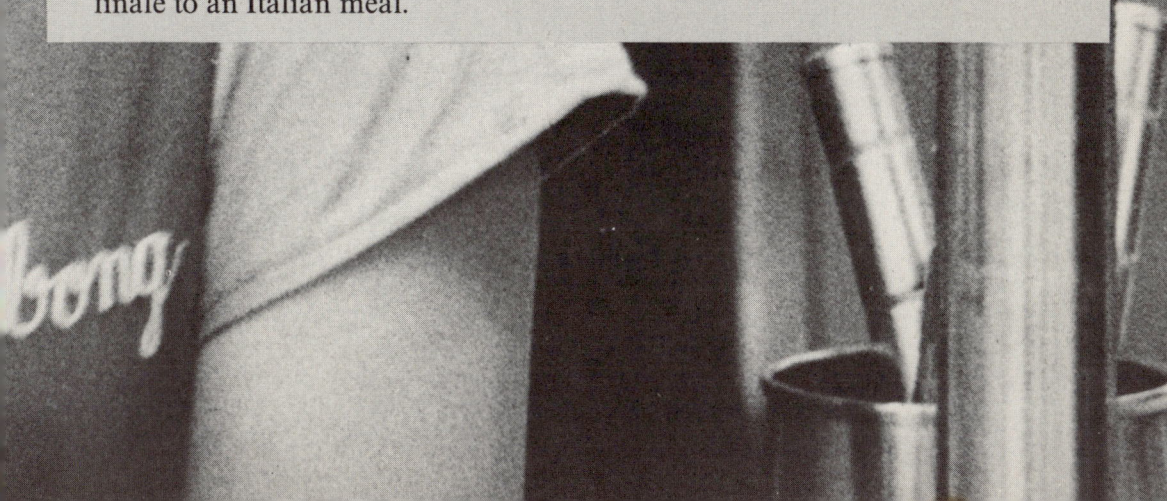

DESSERTS AND CAKES

The Italians have a penchant for glorious desserts and cakes. However, some of them are rather rich.

Italian Pritikin style desserts and cakes have the same mouth watering flavours, but do not contain cream, butter or sugar.

I hope you like the tangy, homemade fruit gelatos.

Platters of freshly cut fruit or a mixed fruit salad is also a very acceptable finale to an Italian meal.

PISA PEACHES
Pesche ripiene

The amazing thing about the Leaning Tower of Pisa is
that it REALLY does lean. I even have a photograph of
myself leaning against it 'propping it up'.

4 fresh golden peaches
1 cup pine nuts optional
1 cup currants
1 teaspoon cinnamon
2 cups marsala

Cut peaches in half and remove stones. Blend together
pine nuts, currants and cinnamon.
Stuff blended mixture into cavity of peach halves. Place
peaches cut side up in non stick baking dish.
Pour over marsala.
Preheat oven to 180°C-375°F.
Bake for 25 minutes and serve.

GRAPE ESCAPES
Uva fresca

This dessert is called 'Grape Escapes' because it's quick
and easy, and helps you to escape from
the kitchen faster.

1 large bunch green grapes
1 large bunch black muscatel grapes
2 cups sweet vermouth

Marinate grapes in vermouth for 2 hours. Drain.
Place grapes in freezer bags and freeze.
Remove from freezer and serve.

Serves 4-6

BAKED RICE PUDDING
Budino di riso al forno

4 cups cooked brown rice
4 cups skim milk
1 cup currants
1 cup raisins
grated rind of 1 lemon
1 teaspoon vanilla essence
2 egg whites
¼ cup marsala

Combine all ingredients and place in non stick baking
dish. Preheat oven to 180°C-350°F and
bake for 45 minutes.

Serves 4

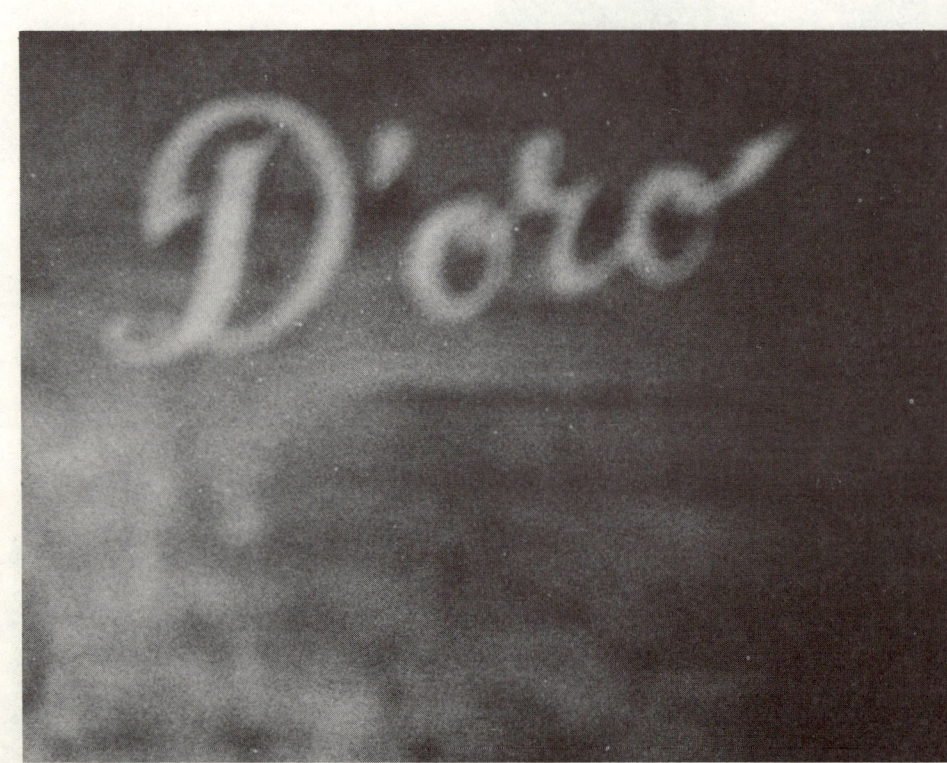

FLORENTINE PLUMS
Prugne stufate

I once spent two weeks living with an Italian family in
Florence – it is a culinary haven. Many people call it
the 'Paris of Italy'. A perfect description!

1 kg fresh ripe blood plums
2 cups red wine
1 teaspoon cinnamon or small piece
of cinnamon stick
Grated rind of 1 orange
Squeeze of lemon juice
2 cups ricotta whip

Wash the plums. Combine all ingredients except ricotta
whip in large saucepan. Cover and simmer for 30
minutes. Remove cinnamon stick. Chill and serve with
ricotta whip.

Serves 6

CHESTNUT MONT BLANC
Monte bianco alle castagne

Mont Blanc nestles on the border between Italy
and France. It is the highest peak in Europe.
This is a traditional Italian dessert to celebrate
this spectacular mountain.

500 grams fresh chestnuts
1½ cups skim milk
1 cup fresh ricotta whip
¼ cup marsala

Slash chestnuts with a sharp knife. Place in a
saucepan and cover with water. Simmer for 15 minutes.
Remove from saucepan and allow to cool. Remove
chestnut shells and skins. Return chestnuts to
saucepan, cover with water and bring to the boil.
Simmer for 45 minutes. Place chestnuts and skim milk
in blender and puree. Spoon into glasses. Top with
ricotta whip, and spoon over marsala. Chill and serve.

Serves 4

PADUA PEARS
Pere stufate

Padua is a short trip from Venice. My mother and I
enjoyed ourselves there shopping, and we had a
delicious lunch at a little trattoria.

6 brown pears
2 cups red wine
1 teaspoon mixed spice
1 teaspoon grated lemon rind
1 cup unsweetened apple juice

Place all ingredients in a large saucepan. Cover and
simmer on low heat until pears are tender – about 20
minutes. Remove pears from saucepan. Spoon over
some of the juices from the saucepan. Serve warm with
ricotta whip, or Pritikin style icecream.

Serves 6

DRUNKEN ORANGES

Arance marinate

4 medium oranges
2 cups unsweetened orange juice
1 cup brandy
squeeze of lemon juice
1 teaspoon cinnamon

Peel oranges. Separate segments and combine with other ingredients. Cover and marinate overnight.

Serves 4-6

ITALIAN BAKED APPLES
Mele al forno

6 granny smith apples
2 cups currants
1 teaspoon freshly grated nutmeg
1 cup unsweetened orange juice
2 cups raisins

Core apples.
Combine currants, raisins and nutmeg.
Puree in blender
Stuff mixture into cavity of apples.
Pour over orange juice and bake in a preheated oven
180°C-375°F for 30 minutes. Serve with Pritikin style
icecream or ricotta whip.

Serves 6

REAL RASPBERRY ICECREAM
Gelato di lamponi

1 x 375ml tin evaporated milk
½ cup skim milk
1 teaspoon vanilla essence
1 tablespoon gelatine mixed with
2 tablespoons hot water
2½ cups fresh rinsed raspberries

Blend or beat all ingredients except raspberries and egg whites until smooth and creamy – about 10 minutes. Pour into icecream trays and freeze for 45 minutes. Blend or beat again for 5 minutes. Fold in whole raspberries and stiffly beaten egg whites. Refreeze.

Serves 4-6

FRUIT SALAD ICECREAM
Gelato d'insalata di frutta

¾ cup skim milk
1½ cups skimmed milk powder
1 tablespoon lemon juice
1 teaspoon vanilla essence
4 egg whites stiffly beaten
1 ripe medium banana
1 kiwi fruit
1½ cups strawberries
6 passionfruit

Peel and roughly chop banana and kiwi fruit.
Remove stalks from strawberries and roughly chop.
Scoop out passionfruit pulp. Set aside.
Blend skim milk, skim milk powder and lemon juice
until frothy. Add egg whites and combine well.
Place in icecream trays.
Place in the freezer for 45 minutes. Remove and rebeat
or blend for 5 minutes. Fold in chopped fruit and
passionfruit pulp. Return to icecream trays and freeze.

Serves 4-6

ROCKMELON GELATO
Gelato di meloncino

1 medium rockmelon
1 cup water
½ cup lemon juice
1 tablespoon gelatine mixed with
2 tablespoons hot water

Puree rockmelon. Add all other ingredients and blend
or beat until well combined. Pour into icecream trays
and freeze for 2 hours. Remove from freezer and blend
until smooth. Re-freeze. Remove from freezer 10
minutes before serving.

Serves 4-6

PEACH GELATO
Gelato di pesca

4 fresh golden peaches
2 cups unsweetened orange juice
¼ cup fresh lemon juice
1 tablespoon gelatine mixed with
2 tablespoons hot water

GARNISH: Fresh mint

Peel peaches and remove stones. Puree in blender. Add orange and lemon juice and stir in gelatine. Pour into icecream trays and freeze for 2 hours. Remove from freezer and blend until smooth. Refreeze. Remove from freezer 10 minutes before serving.

Serves 4-6

BLUEBERRY GELATO
Gelato di mirtilli

An Italian recipe for a 'new' Australian grown fruit

4 cups fresh blueberries
1 cup water
1 cup lemon juice
1 tablespoon gelatine mixed with
2 tablespoons hot water

Puree blueberries. Add all other ingredients and blend or beat until well combined. Pour into icecream trays and freeze for 2 hours. Remove from freezer and blend until smooth. Re-freeze. Remove from freezer 10 minutes before serving.

Serves 4-6

STRAWBERRY GELATO
Gelato di fragola

4 cups fresh strawberries
Remove stalks
1 cup water
1 cup lemon juice
1 tablespoon gelatine mixed with
2 tablespoons hot water

Puree strawberries. Add all other ingredients and blend
or beat until well combined. Pour into icecream trays
and freeze for 2 hours. Remove from freezer and blend
until smooth. Re-freeze. Remove from freezer 10
minutes before serving.

Serves 4-6

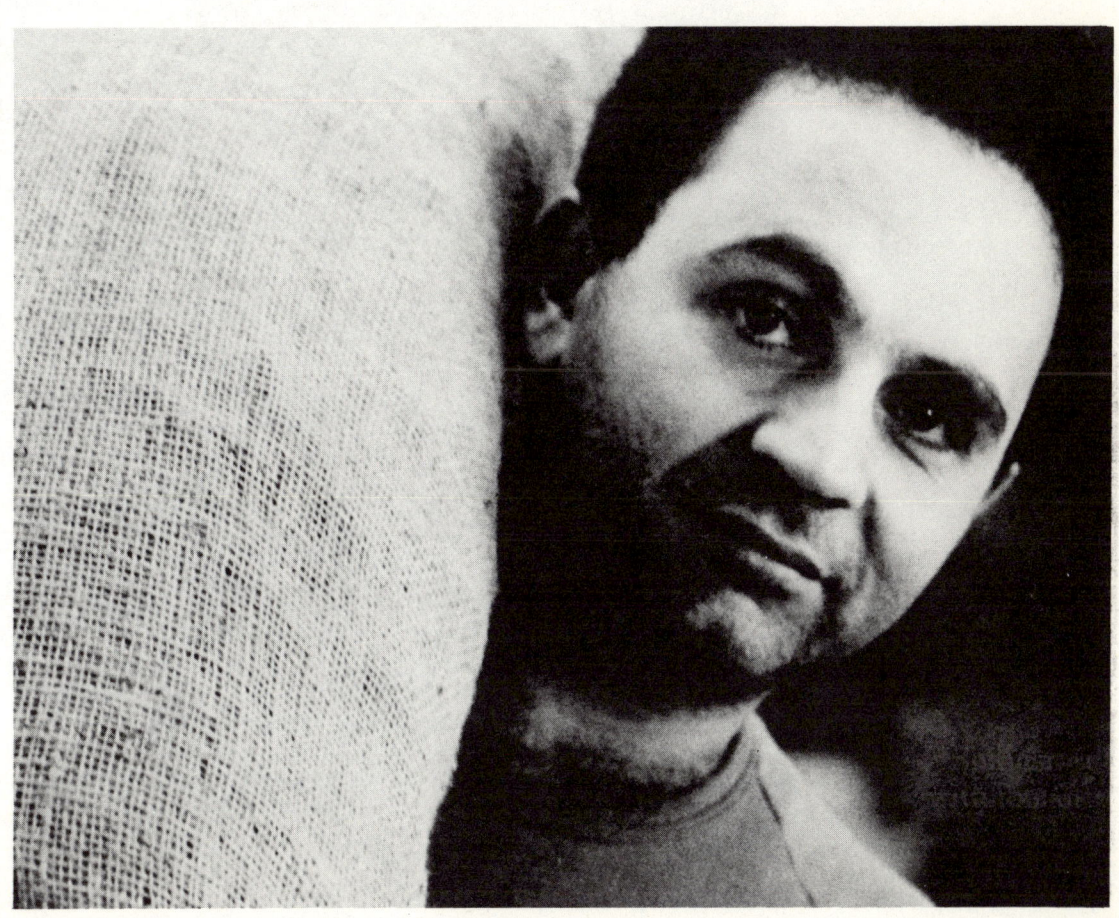

APRICOT FRUIT WHIP

Frullato di frutta all'albicocca

300 ml skim milk
4 fresh ripe apricots with stones removed
1 cup crushed ice
1 tablespoon marsala

Blend all ingredients until ice is well combined.

Serves 4

RICOTTA WHIP

250 grams fresh ricotta cheese
¼ cup skim milk
1 teaspoon vanilla essence

Blend until smooth. Serve as a topping for desserts.
Delete vanilla essence and you have an instant creamy
base for pasta sauces.

PARADISE PIZZA
Pizza dolce

This pizza topping is perfect to serve
with a 'dessert pizza'

250 grams fresh ricotta cheese
¼ cup skim milk
1 cup chopped dried apricots
1 cup currants
1 teaspoon mixed spice
½ teaspoon vanilla essence

Puree ricotta, skim milk, vanilla essence and mixed
spice. Fold in dried fruit. Spread onto uncooked
pizza base. Preheat oven to 200°C-400°F and
bake for 20 minutes.

Serves 4-6

FIG-ARO CAKE
Dolce di fichi e pinoli

The Marriage of Figaro is a famous opera. I hope this cake is famous with your family and friends.

4 egg whites
1½ cups wholemeal self raising flour
400 grams dried figs finely chopped
Rind of 1 orange grated
Rind of 1 lemon grated
1 cup finely chopped pine nuts – optional
1 teaspoon freshly grated nutmeg

Beat egg whites until stiff. Set aside. Sift flour. Combine all ingredients and mix thoroughly. Bake in a non stick loaf tin in a preheated oven 200°C-400°F for 35 minutes. Allow cake to cook in tin. Remove, wrap in foil and refrigerate for 24 hours before cutting.

Serves 4-6

RICOTTA CAKE
Dolce di ricotta

BASE:
1 cup oatmeal
1 teaspoon freshly grated nutmeg
2 tablespoons unsweetened apple juice

CAKE FILLING:
500 grams fresh ricotta cheese – well drained
2 egg whites
1 tablespoon finely grated lemon rind
1 tablespoon finely grated orange rind
1 cup currants marinated in
½ cup marsala for 30 minutes
1 tablespoon gelatine mixed with
2 tablespoons hot water
½ teaspoon vanilla essence

Combine base ingredients and press into bottom of non
stick 20cm cake tin. Refrigerate for 1 hour. Remove
currants from marsala and drain. Add raisins to other
filling ingredients. Beat or blend until smooth and
creamy. Pour into cake tin. Preheat oven to
180°C-375°F. Bake for 40 minutes. Cool.
Refrigerate, slice and serve.

Serves 6

MARVELLOUS MENUS

Below I have outlined some possible menu combinations which may help you plan a family dinner, a dinner party, lunch or dinner for two. The dinner party menus are for 6-8 people. The family and lunch menus are for 4-6 people. Enjoy!

FAMILY DINNERS:

Minestrone soup with wholemeal bread
Wholemeal fettucine with pesto sauce
Mixed Italian salad
Rockmelon gelato

Delicious asparagus
Roast rosemary chicken
Stuffed tomatoes
Pisa peaches

Zucchini soup
Vegetarian supreme pizza
Cauliflower salad
Fresh fruit platter

Tomato and basil soup
Beef in red wine
Baby squash with herbs
Ricotta cake

DINNER PARTIES:

Rennaisance rockmelon
Pavarotti potato soup
Fish feast
Herbed potato croquettes
Real raspberry icecream

Spinach soup
Tagliatelle with tomato and basil sauce
Seafood salad
Figaro cake

Mushrooms with garlic and parsley
Rigatoni with bolognese sauce
Fennel salad
Padua pears

Calabria calamari
Garlic potato crisps
Spinach and ricotta gnocchi
Capri carrot salad
Grape escapes

LUNCHES:

Cauliflower and rice soup

Spinach lasagne
Fresh fruit salad

Mixed antipasto
(Mushrooms with garlic and parsley;
Calabria calamari; Delicious asparagus;
Tuscan tomatoes)
Garlic prawns
Apricot fruit whip

Minestrone soup
Pizza with marinara topping
Mixed Italian salad
Fresh fruit platter

Mixed Italian salad
Spaghetti with tuna and celery sauce
Florentine plums

DINNER FOR TWO:

Tempting tuna salad
Savoury bean crepes
Italian baked apples

Tomato and basil soup
Genoa grilled fish
Steamed green vegetables with herbs
Fresh fruit platter

Minestrone soup with wholemeal bread
Mixed Italian salad
Fruit salad icecream

Peasant chicken casserole
Vegetarian risotto
Pisa peaches

*I*NDEX

ANTIPASTO AND SOUPS

PAGE

PASTA AND PIZZA

VEGETABLES, SALADS, RICE, AND POLENTA